My Tiny Chaotic Universe

JITHU BIJI THOMAS

Illustrated By- Manjula Logendran

INDIA • SINGAPORE • MALAYSIA

ISBN 979-8-89067-903-1

To,

My dear one, **Jelita**. My little sister who has grown up. The only person who keeps calling me 'Champ'. This person is the reason that I didn't give up when I wanted to give up all of it. Her face came up over and over when I stood at the edge. I didn't want to teach her that hope was lost in this beautiful world.

For,

Dhinagar and **Priya** without whom this book wouldn't have been possible. The one line Dhinagar mentioned- "There are people who need you here" was the line that took me back to writing. Writing has and will always be my solace.

Many have helped me keep up my sanity during all the tough times. I can't name all of them because I am scared that the list might miss out on some.

A special mention to Manjula (@manjosfacture) for getting the illustrations done on time.

Contents

From the Author

Hope all of you are doing good out there. Thank you for picking up this book and I promise not to disappoint you. This time, I have tried to inculcate the ideas of existentialism with some witty thoughts and also some great illustrations. The illustrations are just an aid to help you in your imaginative process. **'Sonder'** is all around us. We live in a universe where even the stars have a story that it hasn't narrated. I have tried to listen to a few of those and pen it down. I hope that you too can open up your ears and listen to all the stories that surround you. In a way, I invite you to be part of the chaotic universe that is in my head. Some of the views on 'Religion' and 'God' aren't meant to offend anyone. Those are just some of my childish thoughts flying around in my head. My mistakes outnumber my rights and I do realize that. I guess, all of us have a lifetime to rectify the mistakes. All we need is an open heart. One thing that troubles my heart is the 'Intolerance' that keeps growing in our society. I hope we light the flare of change in our heart and love each other. Let us not let gender, caste, creed or color differentiate us. Evolution has built each one of us to be protective of our clan but it's time to put time and effort and get over it.

Permission

Once I was down with a flu,
I felt left out,
The feeling of dejection was spreading all over me.
I felt very menial in the grand scheme of things,
Do you want to know the reason?
The virus didn't ask me for permission
Before entering my body.
I hope you know what I felt like!

The Universe is our Home

Once my roommate was about
To get evicted from his room,
Money was short on him
But his face did not deny any of feelings that
He carried within him.
When he bid farewell to me,
I couldn't resist but ask the question,
"Isn't it tough to carry the television around with no place to stay?"
He had a witty reply,
"Maybe I can watch the television at the beach when I sleep tonight"

Change of Norms

Let me introduce you to a world,
Where the gods would already decide,
The dress which a child would wear,
When they came out their mother's womb,
The dress decided the caste, creed
And many more variables of the child.
One day a outcast was born among them,
It caused a ruckus in the society,
Everyone felt like their society was falling apart.
The outcast was a naked child after all!

We Will Come Back Home Again

We agreed on the citizenship of the earth,
But my mind whimpers.
The whole earth could be my home,
But I long for that tiny corner,
That tiny corner...
My heart beats a little different.
A little different,
A decipher of the beat may sound like,
"We will come back home"

I Guess I Have the Better One!

Once we lived on the outskirts of a forest,
We decided to please the elephants who
Would pass our way.
We kept a sugarcane hoping to impress the elephant.
The next morning.
A visitor woke us up,
It was an elephant with a gift,
The elephant gifted us some better quality sugarcane from the forest.

What's the Point? They Will Outlive Me!

Gazing out of my window,
I had my thoughts to accompany my worries.
Thoughts upon thoughts piled over.
Then at one point in time,
A bunch of trees caught my attention.
In all probability, those trees were
Going to outlive me.
I was thinking of passing down my worries to the
Tree,
Hoping that,
My worries would outlive me.

An Approaching Freedom

The other day I saw my grandmother,
Her eyes were getting smaller
And skin waiting to detach from their place.
Memory had abandoned her long back.
Only some muffled up words were her companion.
All the while I kept wondering...
Were those words,
Her agony?
Or
The cries of an approaching freedom?

Do I Know You?

We overlooked the counsel of gods,
Each one of them argued about
The greatest among them.
Then the arguments spilled over to,
Who existed first among them?
The rants went on and on...
'Time' made a grand entry without any invitation.
Do you know the funny part?
'Time' wasn't aware of the existence of any gods.

Falling in Love with a Song

We fell in love with a song,
We couldn't resist playing it in loop mode.
Our hearts felt fulfilled,
But at one point...
We thought...
Are we missing out on the next song?
What if the next song was ever better?

Stop Grinning From There

"Did you know that the fishes had spirit?
Well I am dead and this is my spirit talking to you!
Where do I start?
Ending up in 'Fish hell' was a tragedy.
But I can't blame anyone,
It was me who pushed my younger brother to
The bait of the fisherman.
I thought that I had a long life ahead of me
But the accidental 'Oil spill' spoiled all my plans.
I am not fool enough to believe that the spill was accidental.
It was the grand plan of the universe executed through the
Corporate giants!
I have lowered my expectations,
I hope that my brother stops grinning from heaven".

Forgiveness

One cloudy day,
A stranger knocked on my door.
I hesitantly opened the door,
It asked my permission to enter my house.
I didn't want it inside my house.
But I couldn't refuse it either.
It sat on the sofa and asked for my forgiveness.
I burst out into a fit of laughter.
"Who in this fucking wide world wants my forgiveness?"
"This is for you, just for you"

Business Plan

We were getting tired of our
Nine to five job
And decided to be our own masters.
We wanted to be our own master of time and destiny.
So we came up with a brilliant business plan.
A plan that would do great at the cosmic level.
We decided to sell 'Water' to the 'Sea'
To the same 'Sea' that we were sailing in.

Social Change

We had a big argument the other day,
He should have at least respected my age.
I couldn't bear his arrogance anymore.
He wanted to change the rules,
He wanted 'Stone, paper, scissors and then pencil'
He was barely six years old.
I got angry and left.
I had many important things to do.
I had to finish my article on 'Social change'

Letter to Oneself

To my flawed fellow human beings,

This letter is not to justify our mistakes, but this is to soothe our soul.

It's fine my dear, just learn and move ahead. Don't be arrogant or defensive about the past. Calm your soul and move on. After all we are just human beings. Take joy in the chance that life offers you to make mistakes. Again, enjoy being human. Move, keep moving

Regards.

My Faded North Star

I had no fucking idea about the north star.
But I wanted to see her smile!
With hope at its epitome,
I pointed out the brightest star in the dark sky.
We had no idea what was happening!
But,
The star, the sky and the sea bore witness to the magic
That was unfolding.

The Out of Place River

This river did not belong to our place.

We resided in hell and we were the fallen ones.

This river was a part of heaven that did not belong here.

Maybe the god who created our 'Hell' was drunk, when he

Placed the river right amongst us.

Each Star Has a Name

"What are you doing with your life?"
This question didn't haunt me.
I just sat with a cigarette,
Gazing the stars,
I was waiting,
Just waiting so that each star would tell me their name.

Stop Emulating Us

We tried to emulate the stars,
Trying to imitate the constellations,
Our bodies were tangled with each other.
Did we invite wrath upon us,
When we tried to personify the gods?
We weren't sure of the blessing or the curse...
Miles, miles, miles apart......
The stars were light-years apart,
They weren't aware of the formations,
Instead...
The stars looked upon us when we made love,
Trying to emulate us.

The Clouds Bore Witness to Us

When I felt her lips for the first time,
The cloud bore our witness.
Those drops in the clouds met for the very first time,
They felt gay and happy.
I lost her down the years...
I missed her and the same clouds never appeared.
The other day when I kissed another soul,
Those same drops came together to be our onlooker.
After all,
I guess the clouds had their own version of time.

Loopholes

Have you ever fallen in love with loopholes?
The very loopholes in your fate?
The mystic alliance of time and destiny,
That entangles with the unknown.
If you haven't fallen in love yet,
Well the loss is yours!

Was That Love?

Once I was trapped in a tank with a shark,
I was granted one last wish,
I wished to be friends with the shark,
The teeth of the shark disappeared right away.
We spend days, weeks and months together...
We got a bit too close I guess,
The day I decided to leave,
The shark confessed his love for me,
I even saw those teeth growing back again!

Where is Your Home?

For one second,
She pointed left,
The next second she pointed right,
Then she pointed up,
She thought of pointing down,
But before she did that,
She pointed towards my heart.
"That's where it is,
Your home is where you decide it to be"

What's Wrong with My Airplane?

My teacher taught me

How to make a paper airplane.

I smiled.

She smiled.

She said “Airplanes soar across the sky”

But...

My paper didn’t,

Was something wrong with me or the airplane?

Can They Breathe?

We packed our bags,
We looked around for the last time,
The water was already seeping in
And we were getting late.
Our ancestors were buried here
And we didn't want to leave this soil.
But global warming had already skipped across
The textbooks onto our lives.

Stop Lying My Friend

Dear friend,
I have come to a conclusion,
You are a liar,
Blatant liar!
You shouldn't lie for these menial matters.
I see the sun going down the hill every evening
And your house is the other way.
You have no chance to see the sun.
And you still lie about it!

Can I Stay Young?

"Blow the candles, my love"

Pause.

Silence.

"What happened? Are you sad?"

Pause.

Silence.

"I am not sad, I think that I can stay young if I don't blow the candles"

The Light That Never Burns Out

There is that light,
The light which has kept burning,
It's not your light at the end of the tunnel,
It's that special light which has kept us going.
It's that light within us.
Rest assured,
We are hopeful of always having this light,
Leading us to the end of the line.

With Freewill in My Pocket

The clown entered the arena,
He had the script and the mask.
But he also had his freewill.
But the freewill conflicted with
the work at hand.
He wanted to sway away from the script,
But the mask felt heavy.
After all the apprehensions,
He was confident of his skill
And decided to get away with the mask.
But to his horror,
He was fired from his job.

The Inclusion That Failed

One night,
I was haunted by the spirits of my forefathers,
I saw and heard their stories
And I was inspired to start walking on all four limbs.
Going to the office next day seemed a tedious task
But it was 'Inclusion' day at the office,
Where they were celebrating differences among the masses
And I was confident of being included.
I walked into the office on my four limbs
And surprisingly, all were terrified.
Within an hour,
The termination letter was at my desk.
I kept scanning for the word 'Inclusion'
In the letter.

The Gift Which Came Late

I wanted a shoe
And I asked my friend to gift me one.
He told me that he would give one at the right time.
I asked him about the right time
And he told me that it's a secret.
I kept nagging for days, weeks and months.
At last the day came and he bought me a gift.
A perfect shoe for my corpse at the funeral.

Two Stories

The train fizzled by,
One story became two,
The story of 'The one who left'
And the tale of the 'Left behind'
I wanted to narrate the story of the 'Left behind' for
Your feeble mind.
But in the end,
That doesn't even matter
Because your puny mind will wonder where the train went.

The Most Beautiful Time

While chit chatting over a cup of tea,
I enquired 'Time',
About the most beautiful time in its lifetime.
'Time' smiled...
And then told me,
"What you have now is beautiful,
Both the past and future are an illusion.
'Now' is the most beautiful time ever.

Don't Try

Don't try,
In the end to soothe and heal yourself,
Just don't try

(Dedicated to the great man who inspired us to write. Anymore words added will be an insult to his legacy)

The New Song

Would you write me a song?
I have grown tired of the old ones,
The old ones are just pricking my heart,
That's all they do now.
So why don't you write me a new one?
I hope that your pen can last a song
And for some inspiration,
Let's listen to the old songs once again.

Just Blow Again

It's not always that tough right?

(Blow out the candles, blow out the candles, you're too old to be shy)

Just blow and hope that the candles go out,

If not...

Just try blowing once again.

The Drenched Words

"Why didn't you write me a letter

Last summer?"

"I tried writing, but the words were drenched from the sweat

On my forehead"

Is Your Heart Red Enough?

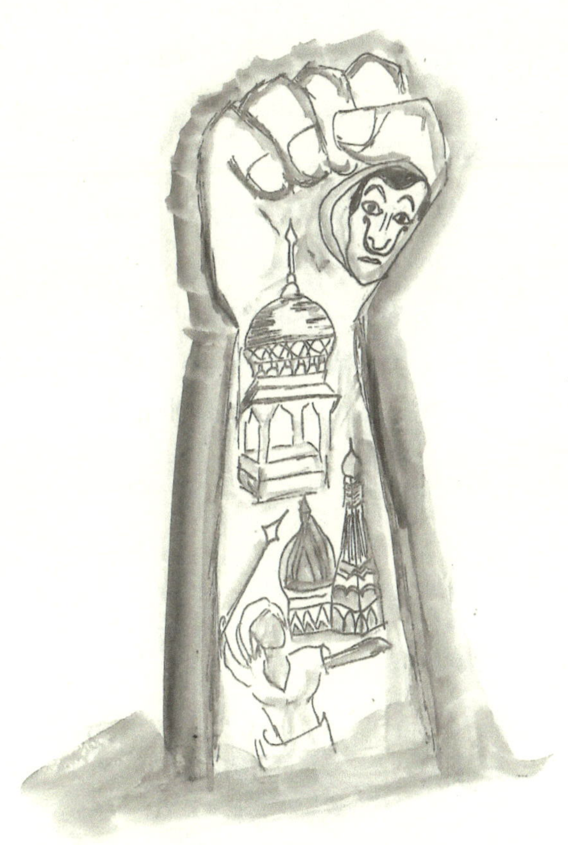

Who am I?
I write my words on any crumbled paper.
But I won't write to soothe your soul,
But I will write for your soul instead!
Yes, my friend!
I have marched in Russia,
I have sung 'La marseillaise' with a clenched fist,
I learnt 'Bella ciao' on the fields of Italy
And even saw the spring in Arabia.
You thought that I were dead
But I was just preparing,
Preparing
To make the sun red again.

The Sleek Wind

Life is sometimes about the

Sleek wind,

That blows on the hottest day.

No Sense of Direction

We made our paper planes,
We aimed in one direction
But it went the other way...
But did we care?
We picked it up again and aimed,
In the end,
We just relished the smiles
And lost all sense of direction.

DUA

It was the end of a much needed vacation,
I wandered about the corridors of the airport,
Pondering on the days that went by.
My parents were getting old and that haunted my soul.
For the first time,
I saw my superheroes vulnerable and that scared me out of my wits.
I was a self declared atheist by this point in my life
But I didn't know where to look for help at this point,
After years,
Many many years,
I told a prayer,
A very silent prayer,
"If at all you are up there, please don't abandon them"
It was my 'DUA' after all.

Dua means invocation - to call out - and is an act of supplication, meaning asking or begging for something earnestly or humbly

My Dear Jack and Jill

Jack and jill went up the hill,
To fetch a pail of water.
Jack fell down and broke his crown
And Jill came tumbling after...
Wait!
Did Jill push Jack?
I guess Jill felt guilty for his act!
That's why she came tumbling after.
Well I don't like spreading gossip either!

Go Around and Around

She asked me for permission,
She seemed modest,
Just like her request.
'Can I go around you?'
I smiled
And mumbled a 'Yes'
She went on and on,
I gave her seasons
And she brought me back memories.
At the end,
I begged her not to stop going around me.
She went on and on...
You knew her by the name 'Earth'
And I was the 'Sun'

The Fallen Leaves

The wind blew
And some of the leaves fell down.
They said “Those are the weak ones”
And they ignored them,
They even left it to rot.
I believed in a world,
Where we would take care of the fallen leaves
Because I was scared of being
The
‘Weak one’.

Ripple

Ripple, ripple, ripple
The full moon was lonely in its reflection
At the lake.
I offered some ally to the moon
But the moon denied it and felt lonely again.
By now,
I wanted someone to talk to
And decided to make a ripple.
I took a round stone from my pocket
And threw to make a ripple in the lake.
Ripple, ripple, ripple
The ripple distorted the reflection of the moon.
I had an evil smile on my face.
But just then,
I had a realization.
I let go of my favorite stone.
And the ripple also passed away.
Now I have a whole lifetime
To decide on what was really important?

The Priceless Paper

Once I went to meet a landlady,
I met her at her home and not at the property
That she wanted to rent out.
There was some sought of arrogance in the air
That hung around her.
I hated the arrogance
But
I wanted some roof over some head.
I swallowed my pride and went along.
When we reached her property.
The funniest thing happened.
The security stopped her at the entrance of the apartment
And told her that her vehicle
Requires the specified sticker on the windshield to enter
The apartment.
I controlled my laughter but couldn't stop smirking.
A paper that worthed less than a penny
Was needed to remind her that
Her appartment was on the earth and not in the heavens.

Stared Down My Soul

My eyes were getting drowsier by each passing second,
I drank for my depression
But I knew that was a bad decision.
Just then...
A lady came and sat beside me,
She stared into my eyes,
Her gaze was so deep that I forgot about everything.
She gazed right into my soul.
Her eyes asked questions
For which I had no answers.
I felt intoxicated,
This time it wasn't the alcohol.
But something that was
Beyond my explanation.
She walked away without saying a word.
But I still keep dreaming of her eyes

The Death Smile

As an angel,
My job was getting weirder as days went by.
I was assigned to gather the list of different types of 'Smiles' that humans possessed.
All went well and fine,
Until I came across one type of smile,
A smile that haunted me down to my bones.
The smile,
The very smile,
That some people gave out when death was at their doorstep.

People

I took a step back and observed it,
The beauty that was just unveiling before me.
The magic called 'People'
The pound of flesh that bled with life.
It wasn't all perfect,
But for the first time in my life,
I wanted to paint.
The chaos, order, mysticity, monotonicity and
Many more!
Out of all this,
When love poured out of each other,
I wanted to be the composer of such music!
The beauty that kept beating within.
Grateful to observe all of this,
I kept on pulsating.

We Will Ride Into Anything

For the first time in my life,
I felt the beautiful pain.
Yes, it is an irony
But the pain was beautiful in all its glory.
I realized a beautiful fact,
It's this pain that makes me feel alive.
My car poked me for attention at this point,
I guess it wanted to be a part of my pain.
I dusted the dust out of my car.
The car didn't complain
But it tried consoling me.
It gave a geekish smile
And said
"Let's ride into many more memories,
Be it happiness or pain"
My beautiful pain started easing out slowly.

May God Help Him

We were stuck at the traffic
And the time didn't seem to move.
A beggar came and knocked on our car window.
I asked my friend,
"Should we help him?"
He gave a witty answer.
"Do what Jesus is telling you right now"
The real concern was that,
I wasn't sure who was talking in my mind,
Was it Jesus or the Mighty Satan?
I decided to listen to the voice
And waved the beggar away.

Who Were the Aliens?

There was a rumble across the night sky,
There were rumors of some aliens,
Approaching our earth.
I was excited
And also anxious at the same time.
The thought of 'We' not being alone
Was soothing.
But how would 'They' treat us
Was still in doubt.
One spaceship landed on my terrace
And a poky figure got out of the ship.
To my utter disappointment,
It pointed at me
And
Said
"Alien".

Louder Than Words

I was waiting for my train
And walking all around the platform.
I was observing people and all their little fanatics.
Most of them were stuck using their 'Smart devices'
And I felt self righteous for not using them.
Just when I was gloating over it,
I saw a man doing a video call over the phone.
He wasn't using any words
But just sign language,
For which the women from the other side of the screen
Replied using sign language.
Gloating gave way to thoughts.
Out of all the commemoration that was occurring
At the platform,
This man's action had the loudest noise.

Get Me a Seat First

One fine morning,
My friend and I decided to take a journey.
A journey to get away from monotonicity.
We were waiting to catch the bus,
When the thought of 'Climate change'
Stuck my mind.
I felt deeply burdened by the thought,
Of our home being uninhabitable.
Just when sorrow and grief were
Overburdening me,
Our bus came
and
A large crowd rushed into the bus.
I did not find a seat
And had to take my whole journey
Without a seat.
I couldn't care any less about 'Climate change'
I wanted a seat first!

www.ingramcontent.com/pod-product-compliance
Lightning Source LLC
LaVergne TN
LVHW091109150826
845673LV00002B/755

* 9 7 9 8 8 9 0 6 7 9 0 3 1 *